Retro Rods

Dan Burger and Robert Genat

MBI Publishing Company

DEDICATION

To everyone who can legitimately say they were there when the original rods and customs ruled the streets. To those who poured their automotive affections into the most personalized, one-of-a-kind automotive creations of all time. And to all the retro-rodders who realize that something very special was happening in American automotive history—it is something still worth being a part of 50 years after the fact.

First published in 2001 by MBI Publishing Company, 729 Prospect Avenue, PO Box 1, Osceola, WI 54020-0001 USA

MBI Publishing Company books are also available at discounts in bulk quantity for industrial or sales-promotional use. For details write to Special Sales Manager at Motorbooks International Wholesalers & Distributors, 729 Prospect Avenue, PO Box 1, Osceola, WI 54020-0001 USA.

On the front cover: A chopped and channeled 1932 Ford three-window, a flathead with straight pipes, and an open road at sunset. Hot rodding doesn't get any better than this.

On the frontispiece: The classic American hot rod has numerous details that distinguish it from its more modern incarnations. A dropped axle, rare Kinment disc brakes, and unique headlights are important retro attributes.

On the table of contents page: Retro rods don't have to be stripped down, bare-bones affairs. This 1934 Ford looks just fine with all the stock chrome trim.

On the title page: If your primered shoebox Ford has flames on the front, it's only natural that it shoot flames out the back. Flame throwers are a popular crowd pleaser at shows.

On the back cover: What could be more natural than a hopped-up Model A highboy roadster under the neon lights of Las Vegas? Every spring, retro rods gather at the Viva Las Vegas car show where primer paint, flames, steel wheels, and unfinished interiors score cool points with fellow retro rodders. Billet owners need not apply.

Library of Congress Cataloging-in-Publication Data

Burger, Dan.
    Retro rods / Dan Burger and Robert Genat.
        p. cm.-- (Enthusiasts color series
    Includes index.
    ISBN 0-7603-0919-1 (pbk.: alk. paper)
        1. Hot rods. I. Genat, Robert, 1945- II. Title. III. Series.

TL236.3 .B87 2001
629.228'6--dc21

Edited by: Amy Glaser
Designed by: Jim Snyder
Printed in China

CONTENTS

I can think of at least two ways that the construction of a book is similar to building a retro rod: The parts come from a hundred different places, and the help of others can get you through some things that you would never figure out on your own.

I'd like to thank several southern California car clubs: the Deacons, Shifters, Choppers, Auto Butchers, and Lucky Ducks. The members of these clubs are building and driving some incredible rods and customs.

I talked to a lot of club members about their cars and the definition and parameters of retro-rodding and then combined it in the best way I could to make this book insightful for those unfamiliar with this corner of the automotive hobby. Those who were particularly helpful include Jonny Guilmet, Morgwn Penneypacker, John Bade, Mick Rossler, Alex "Axle" Idzardi, Johnny "The Ghoul" Greybeck, Mike Ibbetson, Jon "Fish" Fisher, Jeff Vodden, and Tom Branch.

From the "older" generation of hot-rodders, I'd like to thank Joe Reath, John Guilmet, Tom Leanardo, Jim Richardson, and Reid Carroll for their insights, recollections, and observations.

Others who took time to assist me include Rob Fortier, John Logghe, Howard Gribble, Charlie Thorpe, Alan Averhoff, Vince Yamasaki, Ali, Colleen, Paul Rebmann, Chuck Edwald, Don Garlits, Zack Norman, Bill Franey, Aaron Kahan, Sam Davis, Ken Gross, Dennis Mitosinka, and Clyde and Gail Bangiola.

I think a car book without pictures would be worse than a world without hot rods. Well, maybe not that bad, but trust me, neither you nor I would like it. So a big thanks to Robert Genat whose hard work developed into fantastic photos that made this book a true chronicle of retro rod creations.

—Dan Burger

INTRODUCTION

This Looks Vaguely Familiar

If the second time around is better than the first, then what is the third? Hot-rodding offered a second life for many haggard, beaten, thrashed, and trashed automobiles. These cars had been put out to pasture and left unprotected from the ravages of time and the punishments of rain, snow, sun, and wind. Machines that were created for the road, had a purpose, and provided service no longer turned a crank or blinked a light. Rather than allowing these vehicles to sink up to their axles in mud and the engines turn to stone, young men with wild ideas and a few dollars in their pockets rescued them and took them home.

In the course of building their dream machines, these young men made the old cars look young again. They took the feeble and enabled them to run faster than ever. I'm not going to say they healed the sick and raised the dead. That would take a miracle. Hot-rodders aren't miracle workers, but they are definitely hard workers. I've seen their garages. If you listen to the original hot-rodders tell stories for a while, it's a miracle some of them are still alive.

Hot rods have been around for as long as there have been automobiles, but the term only gained widespread use in the years after World War II. Hot-rodding picked up momentum in the early 1950s and then took off like an accelerator pedal stuck to the floorboard. Its popularity was a phenomenon not unlike the rock and roll music popular at that same time. There were people who strongly believed Satan had a hand in both; however, my research discovered no evidence that this was, in fact, the case.

The most striking similarity between hot-rodding and rock and roll was that they each were emblematic of a break from the mainstream. They were anything and everything but ordinary and underscored a desire by those involved to think differently and be different.

That's just one aspect of hot-rodding, however. There was more than one reason for its popularity.

Building a rod or a custom is like putting together a puzzle with some of the pieces missing. It provides not only the challenge of the puzzle but the opportunity to make the puzzle fit the individual rather than the other way around. As a builder you are bound by hard-and-fast mechanical principles on

This channeled Model A roadster was built and driven by Ron and Gene Logghe. The Logghe brothers later gained national recognition for building drag racing chassis. *John Logghe Collection*

one hand, and you are completely free to set new creative boundaries on the other. There is great satisfaction to be found in projects that involve both discipline and creativity. It allows individuality to show, and that's why these cars are some of the greatest automobiles of all time. People poured so much time and effort into them. The hot rod ethic was completely different than the mass-consumption,

standardization of cars. It's ironic that Henry Ford built an empire on that standardized principle, and the rod and custom builders used the same products to create entirely different cars.

The process of building a rod or custom during this era also had the appeal of a treasure hunt. There was little opportunity for off-the-shelf buying. Instead of "I want it, I'll buy it," it was "I want it, I'll build it." Maybe it was the pioneering spirit or self-reliance that came with taking the road less traveled.

The retro-rodders of today exhibit many of those same traits. They appreciate what it took to build a rod or custom in 1955 and recognize the individuality of those cars. It was a highly creative time, and many of those cars vanished from the scene. It's good to see the retro-rodders preserving what they can to build old-school rods and customs that honor the originals. This makes it the third time around for some of those old jalopies. They make sense of funny sayings such as, "It's déjà vu all over again."

This Olds-powered rod was built in Detroit in the mid- to late-1950s. The challenge of building a retro style hotrod is gaining popularity 50 years after originals like this one prowled the streets and strips. *John Logghe Collection*

CHAPTER ONE

When does a rod become retro? The term *retro rod* could easily be considered redundant. After all, aren't all rods retro? That question can be answered "a little bit, yes, but a little bit more, no." It takes a good eye and some familiarity with hot rod history to make distinctions. Even with those skills, the boundaries of retro are open to different interpretations.

Hot-rodding covers a lot of ground. It has always been an experimental speed laboratory most often operating out of the corner of some back alley garage. It began with the dawn of automobile creation. As soon as someone had a car, there was someone else who wanted a car that was faster. Look in the automotive history books. There were always gearheads who wanted to strip down a car body to the bare necessities and build up an engine until it breathed fire, roared like a monster, and set new records for scorched earth.

Although the basic tenets of hot-rodding were in place, the one-of-a-kind, built-for-speed, do-it-yourself customs weren't called hot rods until the wild automotive experience that exploded just after World War II. This particular era—from 1946 until the early 1960s—was the crucible of hot-rodding as we know it today. The cars that were stripped down, the engines that were built up, and the collaborative efforts that went into these one-of-a-kind, home-built, street-and-track racers are milestones in the rich

Take a Model A Ford roadster, drop in some vintage 1960s power—such as a small-block Chevy that was separated from its Corvette body—and you've got a good start toward a retro rod that will win praise and admiration.

Halibrand knock-off wheels are a rare accessory item from the 1950s era. Hairpin radius rods are a classic addition. The owner of this Model A hot rod built his own when he could not a pair one that had the right look for his rod.

American automotive heritage. The cars, technology of that era, enthusiasm for automotive adventures, and the place in this country's history combined to make these hot rods some of the greatest cars to roll down blacktop anywhere.

Exact definitions for hot rods are seldom agreed upon, but the parameters for a modern-day retro rod generally coincide with the hot rods that were created during the time frame mentioned above. The choices for body, frame, engine, and accessories were truly whatever was handy, but certain styles prevailed and certain engines excelled. A combination of supply and demand, trial and error, and throwing caution to the wind produced incredible ingenuity.

The popularity and notoriety of hot-rodding shifted into high gear as America became car crazy in the late 1940s and early 1950s. Because new car production was shut down during World War II, between 1942 and 1945, demand was miles ahead of supply. Even though early postwar production consisted of warmed-over prewar models, the clamor for new cars was like a tide moving in and sweeping the dealers' showrooms clean. With each year after the war, new car production picked up. The used car business was also brisk as many older cars were traded in. These used vehicles, plus the abundance of junkyard iron from the 1920s and 1930s, became the fuel for the hot rod fires.

As America traveled through the 1950s, new car development created a horsepower race that placed an emphasis on power and speed. This was especially true in the low-priced cars where economy had always taken precedence over speed. The mass-market cars developed tremendous brand loyalty, and pride of ownership became increasingly dependent on performance attributes. In addition to that, a growing popularity for auto racing also rubbed off on young people looking for excitement.

Another big reason for the increasingly widespread appeal of hot-rodding during this time was the introduction of the rodding enthusiast publications. The biggest and most well known was *Hot Rod*, a Los Angeles–based monthly magazine produced by Petersen Publications. Along with the standard-sized *Hot Rod* were the

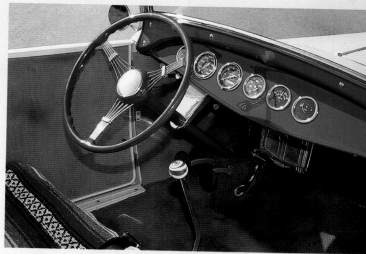

The Model A retro rod interior is simple and to the point. Six gauges provide all the necessary information, interior panels are made of wood, and the small underdash heater box has been chromed. A Mexican blanket across the seats is a favorite southern California accessory.

miniature format magazines such as *Rod & Custom*, *Honk!* (later *Car Craft*), and *Hop Up*. These magazines were filled with photos of the coolest rods and customs along with how-to advice for the growing legion of hot-rodding enthusiasts.

The Hollywood factor was thrown in as hot rod movies became a sure way to attract a teenage crowd to the drive-in theaters. Although the depiction was far from accurate, the big screen put hot-rodding in the spotlight along with rock and roll music.

Find it. Buy it. Build it.

The basic hot rod formula consisted of a cheap, bare bones body and a high-

Attention to detail can go to great lengths. This chopped roadster is a 1950s-style hot rod showpiece. Take note of the beautiful folding top, the drilled front axle, and the 16-inch wheels.

performance engine. It doesn't sound like much, but it prompted creativity to blossom as hot-rodders took a completely different road than the one the major auto makers were on. Factory assembly lines were stamping out bigger, heavier, more luxury-laden and expensive mass-produced cars, and they were selling like hot dogs on the Fourth of July. The hot rods were smaller and more Spartan, but noticeably quicker and more exciting. They were also built to individual desires and funded by part-time or first-job-out-of-school paychecks. Those who could skillfully handle a wrench and a cutting torch took the place of automotive designers and production workers and built the car young America could relate to.

Just about everyone living in 1950s America said Detroit was building the American dream and the hot-rodders were creating an American nightmare. Hot rods were outside the boundaries of mainstream American thinking, and the guys who built and drove them were seen as renegades. That reputation was all the better for those who wanted to break

LEFT

Flathead Fords were the rodders' choice during the early postwar years of hot-rodding. Few were finished as beautifully as this one, which includes a supercharger, beehive oil filter, and custom headers.

away from the herd. The attainment of nonconformist status played a huge role in the enduring interest in hot rods and hot-rodders. A cool set of wheels was the signature statement for those who chose to think differently.

Most hard core hot-rodders probably wouldn't disagree with the nonconformist description, especially if conforming meant having to settle for the assembly-line cars made for the average American family. But thinking outside the box is not, in and of itself, enough to make a worthy hot rod. Hot-rodders were more than renegades. They were also planners, engineers, designers, and test pilots. Within their network of friends, they put together impromptu automotive research and development departments. They ventured out to the cutting edge, pushing development but maintaining self-imposed fiscal restraint. In many cases the most important role may have been the treasure hunter. Hot-rodders picked over the boneyards where abandoned and abused junk lay rusting away. Parked in farmers' fields, an old shed, or sometimes the back row on the used car lot were the bargain purchases that make great stories

A Ford banjo-style steering wheel and Auburn dash add class and clearly differentiate this car from the modern street rods that use billet as brightwork.

even when they aren't mixed with beer and fabrications of the truth.

For a lot of car enthusiasts, the hunt is the best part of getting a car back on the road. It's like being a detective. There are investigations, you chase down leads that are often dead ends, and you find what you want, but you may not be able to pry it loose.

One rodder's story recounts an attempt to buy a 1932 five-window coupe. The opportunity took place 17 years ago when he was in high school. The owner of the car wanted $2,000 for it, and the high school kid tried to imagine where he'd come up with that kind of money. He knew one thing though: He had to have that car. It had the potential to be just like the John Milner car in *American Graffiti*. During the negotiation process the owner decided he didn't want to sell the car. It was an opportunity lost, and these kinds of opportunities don't come around often.

In this case, however, opportunity returned for a second visit. Seventeen years later the rodder returned to see if

Channeling the body over the frame rails was a nice touch that creates a distinctive look, especially noticeable around the rear tires. This red-primered 1932 three-window coupe is also chopped.

Stripped-down cars with built-up engines were usually built on a budget with more money going into the engine and suspension equipment than the cosmetics. This Model A roadster features cool headers, hairpin radius rods, finned Buick brake drums, Buick Nailhead engine, ´32 Ford grille shell, and a Duvall-style windshield.

by chance the car was still around. It was and so was the owner. The rodder says, "I tried to buy this car from you 17 years ago when I was in high school and you wouldn't sell it to me. What do you want for it now?"

"What did I tell you when you were in school?" the owner said.

"$2,000."

"Then it's $2,000 still."

The opportunity to buy that coupe did not pass by the rodder again. He gladly took the deal. "That car was my life's destiny," he told me. "There's no other car I ever wanted."

Salvage Yard Speculations

Most rods of this era began with vehicle bodies dating back to the 1920s, with the majority being factory-built

In-progress street rods are in the majority at retro rod events. Cars like these are driven sometimes daily in areas where the weather permits.

passenger cars from the 1930s. To a lesser extent, certain 1940s- and 1950s-era vehicles are also included in the retro rod family. Getting something cheap was the primary reason for latching on to something that was 15 to 25 years old or older. Hot rod project cars always had more cash (although generally not much more) designated for engines and mechanical components than they did for cosmetic touches. The majority of 1950s-era hot-rodders were rebuilding used engines that ranged from the early 1930s to several years behind the current models. The latest technology and the most modern engines and mechanicals

RIGHT
The radiator guard on this Deuce coupe is a great retro accessory item. Devil artwork is popular with the retro-rodders because it symbolizes a nonconformist attitude.

Open hoods with fully exposed engines are the most common look for the retro-rodders. In this case, a 1960s-era Pontiac tri-power engine is on display.

The bright blue paint and chrome wheels on this five-window coupe give it a late 1950s or early 1960s appearance. Retro-rodders generally believe the early 1960s were the final days of vintage hot-rodding.

made it into only the bigger-budget rods that were comparatively rare.

The remains of Chevys, Plymouths, and Fords have always been particularly easy to find. These cars were produced as basic commodities like bottles of ketchup or pairs of shoes. Long production runs on these mass-produced vehicles made parts interchangeability a better bet when buying a thoroughly worn-out vehicle. If the chosen junker didn't come completely equipped, spare parts could be located easily, or creative adaptations could be fabricated. Knowing what combination of parts worked best was one thing, knowing where to find them was another. In a way it was like mining for gold.

Out in the salvage yard ocean of potential hot rods, the Fords stood out. This was partly due to the sheer number of cars Ford Motor Company let loose on the streets. Model T and Model A Fords once covered the highways like ants on their way to a broken bag of sugar. What truly separated the Fords from the Chevys and Plymouths, which were also cheap and plentiful, was the connection Ford had with aftermarket speed equipment manufacturers. This bountiful relationship began in the days when Ford built only four-cylinder engines. The speed junkies of that era drove cars with stripped-down bodies known as speedsters. Modified Model T and Model A Ford engines were the most popular setup for street and track during the 1920s and 1930s. Chevy and Dodge-powered speedsters were much less common, and performance parts were almost nonexistent.

The Fords were not only an affordable product, they could be upgraded readily to produce a much higher level of performance. The Ford Motor Company benefited from this performance opportunity through the Model T and Model A era. When Ford introduced the V-8 in 1932, the high-performance speed

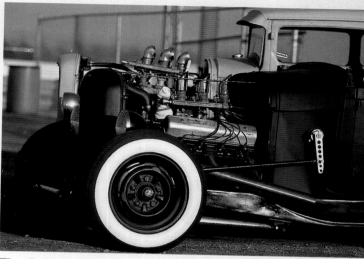

The flathead Fords ruled hot-rodding for many years, but with the introduction of the overhead-valve V-8 by Cadillac in 1949, a change was underway. This Model A roadster is packing an early Cadillac OHV V-8.

equipment manufacturers that had been with them for years followed along.

It's a common misconception that the Ford V-8 immediately claimed the high-performance throne, but in reality the hopped-up four-cylinder engines held their own for seven or eight years until the latter part of the 1930s. Take into consideration that a four-cylinder Ford with one of the aftermarket overhead-valve conversion kits could pump out 100 horsepower, and a factory stock V-8 was rated at 65 horsepower. As the overall economy climbed from the worst of the Depression years and sales of the V-8 Ford continued to rise, more speed equipment was produced

23

and the flathead's popularity as a "poor man's" performance engine skyrocketed.

By the late 1940s and early 1950s, there were millions of Ford V-8s in existence. This resulted in an ample supply of used engines at prices that were easy on the pocketbook. The timing was right for young guys looking to build their own creations and get a lot of bang for the buck.

Although hot-rodding was basically an anything goes endeavor, one vehicle rises above all others when it comes to hot rods: the 1932 Ford, reverently referred to as The Deuce. It has ruled over postwar hot-rodding without ever losing the right stuff. This one-year-only body style is so popular that reproductions, in both steel and

fiberglass, have been produced and sold well for many years. Unfortunately there have never been enough of Deuce body originals to satisfy the hot-rodders' lust.

Deuce roadsters are the most prized body style. Hot-rodders during the 1950s quickly snatched these up because they were lightweight and cheap. In most cases the fenders and bumpers were thrown away because the rodders were looking to reduce weight. If anyone had thought about how expensive those fenders and bumpers would be today, no one would have thrown them away.

Because the design of the 1932 Fords placed the body on top of the frame rails, the rods that retained the stock configuration were known as "highboys." The unique 1932 frame rails make the car a highboy. The term also applies to Model T and Model A bodies that were set on Deuce rails. These bodies were even lighter than the equivalent Deuce roadster, coupe, or sedan, so it became a common hot-rodding practice to take advantage of even greater weight savings of the Model A and Model T Fords. The highboy is a hot-rodding icon, but the 1932 Ford rod comes in many great flavors.

On the heels of the Cadillac and Oldsmobile overhead-valve engines was the Chrysler OHV hemi head engine. At the drags and out on the dry lakes, the big hemis kicked butt. When a hemi showed up in a street rod, it turned heads. This hemi is topped with a log-style manifold and six Stromberg carburetors.

When Flatheads Roamed the Earth

When it comes to retro-style hot-rodding, the Ford flathead V-8s (1932–1953) are the overwhelming choice

Fenderless cars dominate the retro-rodders, but bobbed rear fenders were not uncommon on the original rods. This rod was originally built in the late 1950s. After being driven for several years it was put away and forgotten until it was recently discovered. It still wears its original lime green paint.

for the right look, sound, and feel. In their day, flathead V-8s ruled. Not only were they inexpensive and convenient to find, they were an easy fit into almost any body a hot-rodder had on hand. This was especially true for the numerous Model T and Model A bodies that were available. A hot-rodder was actually making it easy on himself by hopping up the V-8 and dropping it into a T or an A. The V-8 engine wasn't any longer than a four cylinder, so the swap was fairly easy. The V-8 transmission also fit neatly into the older, cheaper models. It was a script that played

The round 1950 Pontiac taillights were often chosen for 1950s-era rods. The license plate lights are another indicator of age. There are not many original rods in this, or any other condition, around.

out again and again for rodders from coast to coast. Mercury engines, a nearly identical cousin to the Ford flathead, were a treasured upgrade commonly seen in the original hot rods as well.

When the Ford V-8 was introduced in 1932, the performance-tuned Ford four-cylinder cars produced more horsepower than the stock V-8. The reason behind this was the number of aftermarket performance parts manufacturers that built equipment for Ford and other four-cylinder cars. Performance parts for the four-cylinder Model A engines were ready around the same time the cars rolled off the assembly line. Hot-rodding still had quite a few stalwarts who believed in the original Ford four-bangers and enjoyed

making a four run faster than most of the new sixes and eights, but driving a V-8 had great allure. Off the showroom floor, the new 221-cubic inch Ford flathead was cranking out 65 horsepower. These engines had 5.5:1 compression and were equipped with a single-barrel carburetor made by Detroit Lubricator. One year later horsepower was increased to 75, and a year after that it jumped to 85.

The Ford flathead remained a 221-cubic-inch displacement from 1932 through 1942, but in late 1938 the famous 21-stud cylinder head was converted to a 24-stud design that would carry through the remainder of its production years. In 1937 Ford introduced the 136-cubic-inch V-8 60—an economy V-8, rated at 60 horsepower, that was produced for four years.

With the introduction of the Mercury automobile in 1939 came a 239-cubic-inch Mercury flathead engine that was rated at 95 horsepower, 10 horsepower more than the Ford. For the short production run in 1942, it was increased to 100 horsepower. After the war, Ford and Mercury shared this

RIGHT
The suicide front axle setup on this sweet little roadster is a cool alternative to the standard dropped axles. This is another original early 1950s hot rod that stayed on the street long enough to go through several updates until it was purchased by retro-rodder Tom Branch who was interested in returning it to its original condition. Fortunately photos exist that will assist his efforts.

A chopped top and big 'n' little tires give this 1932 Ford three-window coupe the profile that rodders of every vintage have fallen in love with. Four rows of louvers and the Halibrand racing wheels make the rod a personal statement.

100-horsepower engine until Mercury introduced a stroked, 255-cubic-inch, 110-horsepower version in 1949. Mercury stayed with the 255-cubic-inch engine until flathead engine production ceased with the debut of the 1954 lineup; however, in 1952 and 1953 the engine was rated at 125 horsepower. Meanwhile the last two years of 239-cubic-inch Ford flatheads were rated at 110.

Flathead fanatics generally agree that the Ford cylinder blocks could be safely bored to 3.375 (3 3/8) without creating an overheating problem due to thin cylinder walls. The prewar Ford flatheads had a factory bore of 3.062, and the postwar Fords were bored to 3.187. Rebuilding a flathead to get the most out of it involved porting, relieving, balancing, and blueprinting. Racing cams, intake manifolds supporting as many as six single-barrel carbs, and performance ignitions were all key ingredients. With high-performance heads the stock 5.5:1 compression ratio could be pushed to 9.5:1. Realistic expectations for these performance-built engines were in the neighborhood of 250 horsepower. More than 12 million Ford flatheads were built during its 22-year run.

The simple red paint used on the wire wheels and grille is an excellent complement to the primer black body and is perfect for a retro rod.

Joe Reath of Long Beach, California, was particularly adept at wringing power out of the flatties. Reath had a reputation on the streets and the strip. Reath Automotive is still a recognized name for many flathead owners who buy parts or have engines built there. As good as Reath is with the flatheads, he's every bit as good at telling tales of hot-rodding's glory days.

Reath remembers buying a 1940 Ford coupe after starting his first job after high school. "I bought it from a guy called The Smiling Irishman who had a car lot on Figueroa Avenue in Los Angeles. The car had 18,000 miles on it, and I gave him $950. The first thing I did was put a set of Smitty's mufflers on it. Everybody had to have a pair of Smitty's. Then I went down to Eastern Auto Supply (later Cal Custom Supply) and bought a pair of fender skirts. On the way home, crossing over a railroad track, one of the skirts flew off and a semi truck ran over it. I'll never forget that."

When Reath started in on the motor, he first bored it out and "played with it a little bit." Then he went to Eddie Meyer's shop and bought a set of heads and a manifold. Those were the early days of what would become a lifetime of adventures on the streets, dry lakes, and drag strips for Reath.

There were, of course, many exceptions to flathead power. Chevy loyalists had high-performance heads and multicarb manifolds available for their inline sixes, and the GMC engine, which was slightly larger and stronger, was not uncommon. Dodge and Studebaker enthusiasts were also among the hot rod ranks. It was a wide-open field with an anything goes just-run-what-ya-brung attitude. The six-cylinder engines developed high torque as a result of long strokes and large pistons, and rodders could take advantage of this by using higher gear ratios. Most sixes could take considerable reboring without nearly the concern for thin walls that was inherent with V-8s. Reboring brings greater cubic inch displacement and with it more horsepower.

Although the aftermarket performance parts industry was heavily weighted toward Ford, there was an expanded effort beyond Ford in the early postwar years. Obviously the manufacturers had come to the conclusion that some rodders would rather drink gasoline than pour it into a Ford, and there was business in some of the other camps.

The 1949 introduction of the modern overhead-valve (OHV) V-8 engines by Cadillac and Oldsmobile set the stage for a new era in hot-rodding. It would take some time to gain acceptance and for old habits to die, but change was on the way. The overhead valve was a smooth-running engine design that immediately raised the performance bar. The extra power and performance, however, came with a higher price tag and a few more pounds to lug around. Two years after the Cad/Olds OHV breakthrough, Chrysler added an overhead-valve V-8 to its engine selection. It established a performance image with its hemi head design. By the time Pontiac and Buick joined the OHV V-8 parade, Ford had the

The retro look favors bias-ply tires in either wide whitewalls or blackwalls with the big 'n' little combination preferred. Steel wheels with baby Moon hubcaps are most common, but spinner-style hubcaps, Moon discs, and old-fashioned wire wheels are also popular.

flathead ready for retirement and began offering an OHV V-8 of its own.

Traditions die slowly. It took several years before the OHV Cadillacs, Oldsmobiles, and Chryslers began to take hold. Even then they weren't commonly seen in hot rods that were built strictly for street use. Those Cadillacs, Oldsmobiles, and Chryslers that did show up in rods got a lot of attention though. The same is true today in the retro rods. A rod with a 331-cubic-inch Cadillac, a Dodge Red Ram, or an Olds Rocket 98 will really draw a crowd.

Full-fendered and without a chopped top, this original ´32 Ford coupe is unique. It was built between 1956 and 1958 and still wears the paint and interior of that time.

A common dilemma for rod builders then and now is whether the engine will fit into the body and frame that awaits it. The hot rod magazines of the period are filled with questions about how to make specific engine, drivetrain, body, and frame combinations work. Issues regarding length, width, height, and weight make some combinations a winning or losing battle. Bigger, heavier engines affect a lot of other components from steering to springs to overpowering the rear end.

Regardless of the technical difficulties, hot-rodding advanced with the times.

Without a doubt the tide was turning, and when Chevrolet introduced its first V-8 in 1955, a monumental shift was about to take place. Chevy's overhead-valve V-8 was both powerful and lightweight. Performance enhancements came on the heels of its debut, and it became a hot rod favorite. Beginning with a 265-cubic inch displacement in two years it grew to 283 cubic inches, and five years later, 327 cubic inches.

Because hot-rodding was inexorably tied to guys with flat rather than fat wallets, cars were usually built with whatever was on hand. Anything that was cheap or free usually had priority status. If that meant building up an inline six, then that's the way it went. If there was a choice, most rodders went with a Ford roadster or coupe powered by a Ford flathead. Ford dominated the scene because it had the low-buck performance edge. First of all, there are two more cylinders than Chevy or a Plymouth, and second, the choices for performance upgrades were far better.

As the modern V-8s became more popular in the mid- to late 1950s, hot-rodding was in transition. Adding to the changing scenery were the postwar used cars that were being chopped, channeled, and lowered along with the traditional prewar hot rod favorites. Late 1940s and early 1950s Fords, Mercurys, and Chevys were out front. High-performance engines remained a primary ingredient, and many of these late-model hot rods were worthy street and track competitors, but many were being modified so radically that they were more of a design statement than a performance tour de force. The customs were displaying a new type of creativity and showmanship born right out of the postwar hot rod scene. It was a way to make an individual automotive statement and to be a gearhead.

n typical late 1950s style, this rod was originally equipped with an Olds J2 engine, and the front suspension is state-of-the-art 1956 Chevy, an uncommon choice.

CHAPTER TWO

The hot-rodders' turf is more varied than any other automotive realm. It's legitimate to say a hot rod is just about anything you want it to be. Distinctions between one type of rod and another are identifiable basically by applications of automotive technology available at any given time. Although modern street rods have a lot in common with the original rods, they are also removed from the original rods by 50 years of technology. Modern street rods take full advantage of the latest advances in automotive science that contributes to more powerful engines, better handling suspensions, more comfort, and convenience. A modern street rod is the natural evolution of a hot rod. Even this description is, at best, a generalization. As has always been the case, some rods are built to go, some are built to show, and many are somewhere on the road between those two points.

The retro rod, however, is a different animal. For the retro-rodder there was an era when the hot rod was perfect. It was pure and raw. Hot-rodding was a special turf where players needed to know the game in order to get in. Retro rods celebrate that era, ingenuity, and the cars that were created. The rods and customs of that era represent devotion and an enthusiasm that was the epitome of what many enthusiasts believe the hobby should be.

Because of the combination of mostly rosy economic and social circumstances in the years

The retro rod style allows latitude for many variations. This 1934 Ford five-window coupe has the quarter windows filled in for a unique look. The car is owned by Alex "Axle" Idzardi, president of the Shifters in Orange County, California.

Oldsmobile's Rocket V-8s were hot throughout the 1950s. They built a solid reputation with the rodders because the engines delivered a ton of torque.

following World War II, hot rods will be forever associated with that technological timeframe. Jobs were plentiful, and America's manufacturing engine was hitting on all its cylinders. Any young buck with an idea, a cheap car, and a little bit of cash could have a hell of a lot of fun building his own rod or custom with his buddies. Before that slice of American pie disappears almost unnoticed, the retro-rodders are pulling it out of history's ditch and putting it on the road again.

Take a closer look at what the retro rods are all about. First of all they are very personal statements. Instead of factories building cars for the masses, these are individual creations. The original hot rods,

and now the retro rods, are what car lovers do when left to their own devices. Most were built with dreams of speed and side-by-side racing, but they also needed to serve as daily drivers. Few factory cars could ever match them when it comes to bold individuality and an uninhibited, unconditional, freewheeling desire for performance and style. For that reason, hot rods rank right up there with the greatest cars ever built in this country.

Recreating the Perfect Rod

To build a retro rod you need to know about the originals. What was used to build them back then is what is used to build them now. Most retro-rodders pick an era, such as the early 1960s, and use few, if any, parts that are more modern than that era. Of course, most of the parts, including the body and frame, were 20, 30, and 40 years old at the time the rod was built in the 1960s.

Hot rods take shape as you build them. That's the opinion of Johnny Greybeck, a member of the Lucky Devils Car Club in Orange County, California. Club members and other friends in the hot rod ranks call him by his nickname "The Ghoul."

The Ghoul and most of the other Lucky Devils drive retro-style hot rods they more or less built themselves. For the most part, the rods are true to the 1950s and 1960s era of hot-rodding. Greybeck's rod is a fenderless 1931 Ford coupe painted with black primer. The 327-cubic-inch Corvette engine is fully exposed. Three Rochester carbs on a Weiand intake manifold stand out at first glance. A closer look reveals homemade headers that Greybeck salvaged from a bucket T that he once owned. He likes them because they have that butchered look that was often seen on personally built hot rods of the 1950s. This machine is both a retro rod and a daily driver. It was built to stand out from the modern street rods and to handle the rigors of day-to-day driving. He chose the 327 Chevy engine because it's more reliable than a flathead Ford. The engine

Anyone with an interest in classic hot rods can appreciate the attention to detail exhibited in this Model A roadster. This is what hours in the garage will produce.

This chopped Model A Ford coupe is a good example of the type of car that attracts the younger retro-rodders. A lot of people between the ages of 25 and 35 are getting involved in building and driving retro rods. This car is owned by Johnny Greybeck, a member of the Lucky Devils.

was bored .060 and makes use of a high-performance cam and roller rockers.

Following the parameters of building rods like they used to, Greybeck put his rod together with genuine 1950s and 1960s hot rod parts and accessories, some of which would have come from bone yard donor cars dating back to the 1930s and 1940s. The front brakes and wishbones are from a 1940 Ford. The shock mounts are cut and altered from a Ford F-1 pickup. The headlight brackets are modified 1932 Ford, as is the front spring, radiator, and shell. A 1936 Ford front spring is used on the rear of this car.

Greybeck fabricated the instrument panel faceplates in an original style. He also made use of a 1956 Chevy ignition switch, a 1949 Montgomery Wards heater, a vintage Klaxon horn, and a steering wheel from a 1940 Ford. The steering wheel includes a customized insert in the center, plus a 1950s-style steering-wheel knob. The BLC aftermarket headlights are a perfect vintage accessory, as are the dropped axle and the Moon fuel block. The coupe body for his rod is from an original car, as opposed to a reproduction body. Reproduction fiberglass bodies are available from several manufacturers. On the Ghoul's car the top was chopped 3 inches. The visor is louvered to give it a definite 1950s hot rod attitude.

The uniqueness of the original hot rods and the lack of documentation on how to build any one rod correctly leaves a lot to the whims of the owner. Photographs from family albums provide a modicum of guidance. Magazines that spotlighted hot rods and customs illustrate many of the finest creations of the 1950s. Before you buy or build a retro rod, a little research is easily and inexpensively done by sifting through the stacks of old magazines at any automotive swap meet.

There are still a lot of the original 1950s-era hot-rodders lurking in the bushes. They have firsthand knowledge of what was on the street and strip. Southern California has always been recognized as the hotbed of hot-rodding, but hot rod roots run all through the United States. In cities, towns, villages, farms, ranches, and lonely rural outposts, hot rods were tops. Like dialects and different ways of waving hello, hot rod styles were regional, demonstrating particular habits and procedures from different areas. It could be favoritism for a particular make of car or engine, a preferred type of exhaust setup, or an approved method of car club identification—such as a plaque in the rear window or mounted below the rear bumper.

A Hot Rod Original

Tom Leanardo of Anaheim, California, is a guy who has been involved in hot rods since the 1950s. He owns a 1932 five-window coupe and a 1936 pickup built in the retro 1950s style, plus he owns several other rods and miscellaneous hot rod parts. Leanardo tells stories about buying these cars back in the 1950s and early 1960s when the 1930s-era cars and trucks cost as little as $20. If you paid $300 that was a lot of money for what most people considered "just an old car."

Leanardo grew up hot-rodding. He picked up cues about how to do it from guys who were building speedsters a

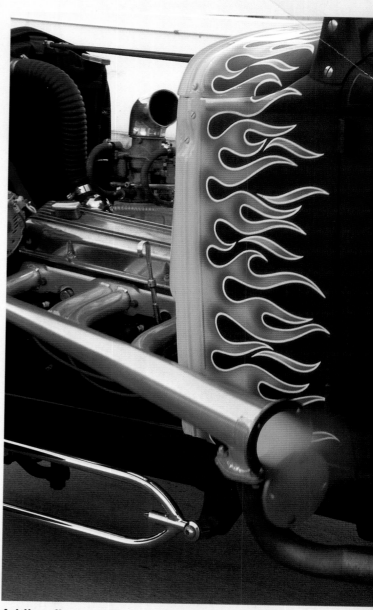

Building a rod according to personal preference appeals to many enthusiasts. Choose whatever steering wheel, instrument panel design, and other accessories you prefer as long as they're not more modern than the rest of your rod.

Adding flames to a rod requires an artist's touch. Styles vary and have evolved over the years along with the paints that are used. With a retro car you don't want to go too far into the future with a paint and flame style.

Many of the original hot-rodders are still involved with building cars the same way they always did. This 1934 Ford sedan, built by Clyde Bangiola, looks like a bone stock factory original, but under the hood is a muscled-up flathead. The extremely rare set of 1930s-era General Jumbo 14-inch wheels are a classy accessory.

generation earlier. His father was a neighborhood pal of hot rod legend Ed Iskenderian and Iskenderian's hot rod friends. Those connections gave Leanardo the opportunity in 1971 to buy an original condition Model T speedster that is a classic prewar hot rod and a virtual twin to the car Elvis Presley drove in the 1957 movie *Lovin' You*. Leanardo has numerous photographs of the car that were taken shortly after the close of World War II that identify many of the unique components, and he can recite the stories of Iskenderian and others who remember the car on the street.

The rod has received some cosmetic attention to restore cracked paint and upholstery, but it remains essentially as it was built. When rodded in 1939, the body was modified very little, with one noticeable feature being a filled cowl. Another popular customizing feature of that era, and the postwar era as well, was dropping in the handsome instrument panel from an early 1930s Auburn. A 1938 flathead with Stromberg carburetors provides the power, and the headers were handmade from Model A exhaust pipes cut and welded together. The wishbone suspension is a neat trick considering it was 1939. Under the skin a cage was fabricated to strengthen the body.

Other items used in this early hot rod were airplane-strut headlight mounts, 1939 Ford taillights, a license-plate light customized from a Mercury, and the front end from a 1936 Ford, which was considered a good idea then. The steering box is from a Willys and the dual-coil set up was from a Lincoln Zephyr. The door handles are from a 1935 Ford.

Leanardo, and many other guys who built and drove their own rods during the 1950s and 1960s, are entertained by and enthusiastic about the younger people who have taken an active interest in retro rods. When he was a kid Leanardo says building hot rods was the cheap thing to do. A generation later, his son builds retro-style hot rods as a business.

Keep Your Eyes Wide Open

Tom Branch is one of the young guys who developed an interest in retro rods. After being involved in hot-rodding for a few years, he became more and more interested in tracking down a car with some hot rod history. It was 1996 when he caught sight of a funky 1970s-style rod for sale at a cruise night in Downey, California. After just one look, Branch realized the rod was suffering from owner neglect and recognized it as an older rod because of the unique hairpin front suspension and a

Twin carburetors on an Eddie Meyer high-rise manifold make sure this Ford V-8 isn't starved for fuel. This beautifully detailed Ford flathead is dressed for show, but it's got plenty of hot rod get up and go.

327-cubic-inch Chevy engine. The car was definitely old school and not the kind of stuff most rodders were into at that time.

After doing a little bit of detective work, he identified it as a *Car Craft* cover car in 1964. At that time it was equipped with a 409, four-speed, slicks, and chrome reverse wheels. He also discovered the car had a movie role as the James Darin car in *The Lively Set*. Even with that interesting past life, the car had more secrets to tell from an even earlier hot rod experience.

Branch tracked down previous owners and found out the car was also on the covers of *Hop Up* and *Hot Rod* magazines in 1952. At that time it had a track nose, Duvall windshield, a Ford flathead, and a 1939 Ford three-speed transmission. It was also exhibited at a car show at the Pan Pacific Auditorium in 1952, one year after it was

This is more proof that a retro rod can fit many descriptions: Only the lowered stance of this 1933 coupe hints at the hot rod beneath. Notice the nice contrast between the apple green wheels and the black primer.

built by a renowned East Los Angeles hot rod and custom shop run by Al and Gil Ayala. Back in the 1950s the Ayala brothers were part of a car club known as the Auto Butchers. Coincidentally, the East Los Angeles car club that Branch belongs to today is the same Auto Butchers club.

By piecing together the rod's past, Branch traced a lifetime of continual alterations. Similar to everything else, fashions change. In the 1960s the track-nose was no longer popular so it was discarded. Not surprisingly, as the car

aged, it suffered the ravages of owner abuse and neglect. When Branch found it, the interior was upholstered in black corduroy. The original instrument panel, a rare Stewart Warner layout called the Straight Eight, was gone and a wood-grain dash had replaced it. Like any restoration project, there were many things requiring attention in order to return the car to something resembling its 1950s origins. The Model A radiator shell was part of the 1970s look that Branch wanted no part of, so he swapped it for a Deuce shell.

There were a lot of home-built rods put together with ingenuity and scavenged parts. In the retro rod world these are the rat rods. Building a rat rod is like preparing a meal with leftovers. There's nothing to say it won't turn out good.

Underneath the body, the wood structure was a vintage 1950s repair of an original wood framework. And although the rod looks cool with its open-hood style and tri-power 327 gleaming in the sun, Branch's desire is to return the rod to its 1951 configuration with a flathead and a quick-change rear end. Like any hot rod or any restoration project, Branch's rod is a work in progress.

Paying Attention to Details

Building a retro rod requires attention to detail just like the restoration of a bone-stock factory original car or truck. Even though a 100 percent authentic job may not be the objective, a few mismatched items can look as out of place as a welder in a French maid's outfit. Most retro rods don't just look the part—they're retro inside and out. Yet some latitude is given if the attitude is there. Occasionally a modern engine or modern automatic transmission is slipped into rods and customs that otherwise are true to their 1940s or 1950s roots. The owners of these cars don't pretend their cars are something they're not. If the rod or custom is otherwise detailed with vintage parts and style, the owner may be cut some slack, especially if he or she is committed to the hobby. Posers, those who pretend to be interested in hot rods, are judged more harshly by the enthusiasts.

Engines and speed played a big role in the original hot rods. The customs were more about show than go, but the engines still were juiced beyond their factory qualifications. Retro rods tend to be drivers rather than racers, but that doesn't mean they can't burn it up. Regardless of the era and the technology, the process of hopping up engines begins with three basic points:

fuel delivery, valve timing, and exhaust.

Multiple carburetors were always one of the first items to get attention when building a rod. Because they sit right up on top of the engine, they make a statement about a rodder's intentions. Maybe you can't judge a gunfighter by the size of his gun, but it's a pretty good indicator of how serious the opponent is.

It was a widely accepted fact that stock engines were starved for fuel. Rods running flatheads and six-cylinder engines always were upgraded to at least two two-barrel carbs, and three, four, and sometimes more were commonly put to

The general guidelines that apply to building a retro rod are also adhered to when working on a rat rod–build it like the rodders would have back in the 1940s and 1950s. This roadster body started out as a 1937 Dodge pickup truck cab. Note the unique headlights and the '34 Ford grille shell.

use. Stromberg 97s on a Ford flathead were just about as common as packs of cigarettes rolled up in T-shirt sleeves. With the overhead-valve engines, the smaller engines such as the Chevy 283s and 327s often took advantage of the three deuces setup, while the bigger displacement engines (most often more than 330 cubic inches) went with a large four-barrel or dual quads. A few of the high-performance junkies experimented with superchargers, but it was relatively rare on the street.

Working in conjunction with the high-volume fuel pumpers were the high-performance camshafts. Standard cams were designed for operation at fairly tame rpm ranges, but speed equipment companies such as Winfield, Potvin, Iskenderian, and Smith-Jones were well-known for their cam grinds that improved valve timing when the engine was running wide open. At a slow rpm these cams were readily distinguishable by the extremely rough idle. The lopey rumble of an engine equipped with a high-performance cam could generally draw sideways glances from the street racing guys who cruised the local hangouts.

Obtaining more horsepower without showing it has its advantages when it comes to racing. Larger valves and lightweight valvetrain components usually accompany the installation of a performance cam. Porting (opening up the intake and exhaust ports) for more efficient airflow also helps squeeze out a few more horses. Polishing the valves, valve surface area, ports, and chambers are other methods of coaxing more performance.

Higher horsepower is frequently sought through higher compression. The first step in that direction is to mill the surface of the heads. The goal is to obtain a compression ratio of between 9.5 and 10.5 to 1.0. At this ratio, it is still possible to use common premium grade gasoline. The 1949 to 1951 Olds engines can be milled .100 of an inch, which is substantial, but it is more common to mill between .040 and .060.

A sweet-sounding engine was also high on the list of importance. Dual exhausts were a must, and the coolest engine tones came from Smitty's mufflers. Mellow-tones and Hollywood mufflers were also highly regarded for their quality, low-throated rumble, but for performance-enhancing power, headers were the answer. Headers are designed to get rid of exhaust gases faster, and their efficiency could boost horsepower by 5 to 10 percent. The design was either straight pipes or a twisted cluster known as a "bunch of bananas." It wasn't unusual for rodders to manufacture their own headers and the open-hood retro rods that are dressed out with these get extra attention. With a fully exposed engine, headers and a multiple-carb setup were an important signature for any rod.

A rat rod takes advantage of whatever works, might work, and can be made to work. What appears to be random and reckless actually is somewhat methodical. This roadster pickup has logged thousands of miles. The red fuel lines are an authentic 1950s accessory item. This car was built by Jonny Guilmet of the San Diego-based Deacons car club.

Power Packed and Race Ready

Although Ford flatheads power more hot rods and customs than any other engine, the early Oldsmobile Rocket V-8s are probably the next most popular. They came on the scene in 1949 about a month after the first Cadillac OHV engines. Due to their compact size, they were an easy fit for many chassis. Low-end torque, a hot-rodding essential, was their specialty due to a big bore and short stroke. The original displacement was 303 cubic inches. Higher compression heads came in 1952, and Oldsmobile increased the bore in 1955, which took displacement to 324 cubic inches.

A stock Olds V-8 in 1949 was capable of churning out as much horsepower as many of the hopped-up flatheads were putting out, and the manufacturers kept pouring it on. According to Oldsmobile sales literature, from 1949 to 1956 the factory Olds engine increased from 135 horsepower to 202 horsepower. The credit is easily traceable to bolt-on speed parts. Any rodder who had the early Olds engine could easily corral the same horsepower gains by following the same moves the factory was making. In the mid-1950s, when one of the new Oldsmobile 88s was hauled off to the junk yard after a wreck, there was probably a hot-rodder there waiting for it to arrive.

The most potent engines of the early to mid-1950s were the Chrysler hemi motors, including Dodge and DeSoto. The high-performance racing guys were winning

A hand-built tubular steel grille insert provides a distinctive appearance to the often-used 1932 Ford grille shell. Rocket Olds 88 emblems on the sides of the cowl let everyone know what's running this rod.

big with these at the drags and on the dry lakes. Rarely will a retro rod be running one of these, but when one shows up it is guaranteed to attract some serious attention. Although speed equipment was readily available, these engines were always expensive. Big demand and short supply will do that. If you were lucky enough to find one and had the bucks to buy it, then you had to wrestle with the size of the engine. These engines are wide and almost always required some creative cutting on frames and bodies to get a good fit.

The overhead-valve Cadillac engines of the 1949–1951 vintage, much like the Oldsmobiles of this time, are also held in high regard. Packing a Cad engine into a rod was an impressive sight, especially when it was crowned by dual-quad carbs. Cadillac made many performance improvements throughout the 1950s as the horsepower race heated up, and virtually every one of them was easily retrofitted to the original OHV V-8s. The reputation of these monsters was built on ruggedness, dependability, and a decent power-to-weight ratio.

As popular as the flathead Ford engines were for the first 10 to 15 years after World War II, the mid-1950s debut of the Chevy V-8 was a hot-rodding milestone. Prior to the Chevy V-8 most Chevy performance enthusiasts chose the 270-cubic-inch and the 302-cubic-inch GMC six-cylinder engines to get more power than the smaller

Vintage 1958 Chevy taillights are not the typical rod selections, but they are in keeping with the overall 1950s theme this owner has chosen.

Chevy sixes would deliver. The 265-cubic-inch V-8 engines changed everything. The change wasn't immediate, but the ripple effect had begun. After two years the 265 was replaced by the 283. In the minds of many people the 283 was the best engine ever built. It was a smooth-running, inexpensive unit that could be hopped up to outperform engines of much larger displacements. The high-performance aftermarket businesses raced to get a piece of this action. Chevy enthusiasts finally had the punch to go toe-to-toe with Ford. During the remaining 10 years of the classic hot rod era, Chevy slowly took control of the fight.

After the 283 came another great Chevy engine—the 327. In factory Corvette trim or with the Power pack option on a standard Chevrolet, these engines made the term

This roadster is an example of the diversity of cars in the retro rod field. Although it looks like a show car, owner Bill Franey says, "I built it because I want to drive it. If you don't drive it, what the hell good is it?"

This metal-flake blue Deuce roadster is being restored as a 1960s-vintage retro rod. It's brightly painted, uses a lot of chrome, and wears cheater slicks. Radir wheels are a personal preference of the owner and are extremely rare.

factory hot rod commonplace. They were the reason a lot of 1955–1957 Chevys were starting to line up next to the traditional hot rods on the street and at the drags. They also found their way into many of the 1930s-era Ford roadsters and coupes. With the performance technology of the era, these small-block Chevys just flat-out ran like stink. They were the modern flathead because they were plentiful, didn't take a rich daddy to buy, and the hop up goodies were readily available.

Hard on the Gears

Getting the power to the rear wheels was sometimes challenging. During the late 1940s and early 1950s, all rods were shifted with manual transmissions. The choices were floorshifts (mixing sticks) or column shifts (mixmasters). As engines were tuned for higher performance,

drivetrain components started failing faster than shop students in algebra class. Gear jammers gravitated toward transmissions that could take the punishment. The solution to that problem was Cadillac and LaSalle transmissions. These transmissions became junkyard treasures because they had a reputation for being strong and dependable. The floorshift 1939 Cadillac side-shift gearbox had many fans in particular. Cadillac standard transmissions all the way to 1950 were popular among rodders.

Rods running flatheads often ran Ford transmissions and rear ends, but the preferred upgrade was the 25- and 26-tooth

configurations were prone to blowing up. A better transmission choice for the Chevy enthusiast was to use the 1936–1941 Packard transmissions from the junior series Packards. Not only was it an easy installation, but the gear ratio was similar to the 26-tooth Zephyr box. Old Packard gears were cheap to buy in the mid-1950s and the rodder had his choice of using the

A no-frills rod couldn't look any better than this. Take a 1932 coupe, strip off the fenders and running boards, lower it, and add some pop under the hood and drop in stylish red and white pleated interior.

Immaculate restorations and recreations of 1950s-era hot rods have led to recognition of these cars at prestigious car shows such as Pebble Beach. The Antique Automobile Club of America has also established a new judging classification for American hot rods.

the reckless built hot rods without upgrading to hydraulic (juice) brakes. It was a frequent upgrade. Therefore, kits were manufactured that allowed juicers to bolt right up to the original spindles.

Brake technology improved dramatically in the 1950s, yet it was considered inadequate when it came to high-performance situations. More than a few people who work on cars of this vintage still don't trust the factory brakes. Those who are not so concerned say the weakest link in the braking system has always been the linings. Modern linings have significantly improved old hydraulic brakes. The debate continues, but the use of hydraulic drum brakes on light vehicles, such as hot rods, does not appear to be troublesome. Those who remain unconvinced won't go with anything less than disc brakes, but they won't win many admirers on a retro rod.

Heat is the enemy of drum brakes, and the 1950s rods sometimes were fitted with finned drum brakes to help cool them off. They are a rare item today and something retro-rodders love. Most were used in racing where the improvements were obvious. Reducing the temperature around the drums had a direct and positive effect on braking by reducing fade. Other techniques include drilling holes in the backing plates and fabricating scoops that duct air through the brakes. Aluminum drums were an advancement in keeping things cool, but few were made. Buick was one manufacturer that used bonded aluminum brake drums. Retro-rodders have their "parts radar" dialed into these.

Most of the original hot rods were driven hard and put away wet. They were lucky to survive the short-term service requirements they performed, let alone the test of time. It makes the genuine article a rare find and a treasure hunter's prize.

Occasionally a rod is discovered. It may be a 100 percent original hot rod, or it may have suffered through some butchering during its lifetime, so it's hard to identify when it was originally built. Bodies, frames, engines, speed equipment, and assorted accessories are still out there to be found. There is a small but growing number of enthusiasts looking to save those hot rod treasures before they rust away or are thrown in the crusher.

CHAPTER THREE

Traditionally customs have been about changing the factory appearance of a vehicle. The expectations are to create an appearance like nothing else on the road. Some owners prefer the highly accessorized look and fully loaded their rides with every conceivable item the factory, dealer, and aftermarket manufacturers produced. Other owners chose to strip the car naked, removing every trace of brightwork except for the grilles and bumpers, to come up with a minimalist design that said less is more. Taking the big step from mild custom to wild custom involved extensive metal work to chop the tops, channel and section the bodies, and, in many cases, completely disguise the make and model of the vehicle.

Redesigning stock automobile bodies into custom cars has been rediscovered by today's youth. The customs of the late 1940s and early 1950s are back on the streets again, often piloted by people in their 20s and 30s. Slammed Mercurys, Fords, and Chevys, with that sinister and sensual nonconformist style, are playing a big role in relighting the rod and custom flame.

Like hot-rodding, the early postwar customs have a heritage that is closely aligned with the 1930s and include roots that date back to the early days of the automobile. During the 1920s and 1930s luxury cars were usually the benefactors of talented metal shapers and upholsterers. Cars such as Duesenberg, Packard, Cadillac, and Lincoln—owned by folks with

Up front, the Chevy grille, DeSoto bumper, and frenched headlights work together beautifully to provide a unique appearance for this retro-style custom.

Mercury wears the crown as king of the customs because of the 1949 to 1951 models. There are other great Merc customs and tremendous sleds from across the automotive ranks, but these are the tops.

A radically chopped top and toothy DeSoto grille are two custom touches that give this 1951 Merc the sinister appearance that captures attention wherever it cruises. This particular Merc is in well-preserved original condition.

deep pockets—were given the custom treatment by coach-building companies with reputations established on unique design and excellent metal fabrication skills. But by the end of the 1930s, most of these shops were out of business and this high-brow customizing was seldom seen. These big-dollar customs are highly prized by classic car collectors.

In the late 1940s when the good times began to roll again after more than four years of war, customizing was reinvigorated. This time, however, it was more closely aligned with cars affordable to the working

class. The auto factories were not back to full production after years of producing for the military, and the public was hungry for new automotive excitement. The circumstances provided custom shops with an opportunity to show how they could restyle and modernize used cars into something special. Mid-1930s Fords made particularly good customs, and the most popular of the prewar customs were the 1936 Fords. With a chopped top, louvered hood, dropped front end, ribbed bumpers, and a molded-in Packard grille, this car was (and still is) the bomb. The 1940 Fords were almost as popular as the 1936, although it should be noted that popular is a relative term.

Jon Fisher is a member of the Choppers, a Burbank, California, club. He owns several

Frenched headlights, shaved hood treatment, custom bumper, Buick wire wheels, and Appleton spotlights are all classic elements that make this custom an American icon.

retro-style rods and customs, and one of his cars is a 1936 Ford coupe customized in the early postwar streamlined style. It's a unique design that is influenced by a custom, owned by Jack Calori, that appeared in magazines shortly after it was completed in 1948. Calori's car also started with a 1936 Ford coupe. In customizing his car, Fisher added a 1939 LaSalle grille, and 1940 Buick headlights. Like Calori's car, Fisher chopped 3 inches from the top, which visually added length of the hood. It's raked in the front and dropped in the back "motorboat style." It's a very futuristic style for that era. The taillights have been removed from the fenders and were built into the 1941 Mercury bumper guard.

In addition to having a sharp eye when it comes to recognizing the talent that went into the original customs, Fisher put some of his own ideas into the car. For instance, he liked the look of the Lincoln Zephyr dash and instrument panel. He found the Zephyr dash, which was ultimately used in his custom, lying in the mud at a swap meet. It required some adapting to fit in the Ford, but the result is retro cool.

Maybe other customizers used this Zephyr dash idea and maybe no one did, but Fisher made it work in his car. It fits in well with the overall retro customized look he gave his prewar Ford. Like most other retro rods and customs it shows an attention to detail that is historically correct. He also chose the wheels, tires, steering wheel,

From the prewar era, the 1940 Ford coupes were excellent choices for customizing. The smooth body shape is accentuated by a mildly chopped top and fenders molded into the body.

seats, and the interior and exterior colors based on research about what was being used in the late 1940s. Within those guidelines, Fisher allows some leeway for simply what he thinks looks good.

Another detail uncovered in Fisher's research was moving the gear selector to the left side of the steering wheel, which was done so that shifting could take place without the driver taking his hands off his date. Nice touch. It reminds Fisher of an old saying, "Customs are for gettin' the gals. Hot rods are for forgettin' about the gals."

Moving into the mid-1950s, the used cars most likely to become customs were the 1949 to 1951 Fords and Mercurys. The same vintage Chevys, Cadillacs, Oldsmobiles, Buicks, and Pontiacs were hot custom selections as well, especially the fastback body styles. Most customs were made from five- to eight-year-old used cars, so as the rod and custom era progressed into the late 1950s, the mid-1950s cars became the customizers' favorites. Fords and Mercurys still ruled, but Chevys were a close third. After that it

Most customs were built for looks rather than speed, but some had a lot of hot rod in them. This 1938 Ford is painted in a style reminiscent of the early postwar dry lakes racers. It has recently turned in 140-plus miles per hour on lake-bed runs.

was anything goes with cool tricks being worked on cars of every description.

Low, Lower, Lowest

One of the most difficult customizing techniques was chopping the curved tops that were used on coupes and sedans of the mid- to late 1930s, and the fastback rooflines of the late 1940s and early 1950s. Chopping the top lowered the roofline, usually between 2 and 5 inches, and produced a more streamlined and

aerodynamic shape. The process involved the removal of a section of the roof support posts and the reattachment of the roof on the shorter supports. It was a fairly straightforward operation on vehicles of the 1920s and early 1930s when the roofs were square with the bodies, but as cars became more streamlined and the roof pillars more curved, the chopping process required greater skills to complete it successfully.

Only so much chopping could be done while maintaining an attractive sense of proportion and design. Windshields and rear windows were especially difficult to resize appropriately, and all the window glass needed to be trimmed accordingly when inches were taken from the roofline. Depending on the height of the driver and passengers, adjustments in seats might have been be required to maintain adequate headroom.

Because automotive design always favors a low car when it comes to appearance, the process of channeling a body gained popularity. Nearly all cars are manufactured with the body mounted on top of the frame. When a car is channeled, the body is removed from the chassis and lowered around the frame. To accomplish this task, the floorboards are cut out and the body is lowered down over the frame. Afterward, the body is fastened to the bottom and sides of the frame. There is a direct relationship between how far the body is channeled over the frame and how much higher the floor pans and drive shaft tunnel are positioned when they are rewelded in place. A new seat structure is required to enable the occupants to remain in somewhat comfortable positions since the floor is closer to the roof.

Lowering the body on prewar cars, with fenders separate from the body, brought the fender line closer to the top of the hood and trunk. This accentuated the lowness of the car and gave it a more modern appearance. Some cars can be lowered as

Louvered hoods were a popular touch for both rods and customs in the early 1950s. The roof on this car was already chopped when the current owner found it in the weeds.

much as 10 inches after channeling, which alters their appearance dramatically.

A third customizing method of lowering the body is referred to as sectioning. It is the most difficult to achieve correctly and is accomplished by cutting out a section of the car body below the beltline. In other words, there were two parallel horizontal

These in-fender taillights originally belonged on a 1941 Studebaker. The bumper-mounted taillights were an aftermarket accessory item. DeSoto bumpers were popular because of their ribbed styling.

cuts around the car, 3 to 4 inches apart. After removing the cut-away metal, the top and bottom halves of the car were welded together. Moldings frequently hid the seam, but with extra effort the seams were welded and smoothed.

Body sectioning was never as common as chopping and channeling, but when executed correctly it lowered the car and gave it dramatic new proportions that clearly set it apart from the crowd. Not only did sectioning create a lower profile, it also saved the headroom that chopping the top forfeited. Because of the original slab-sided design of the shoebox Fords, they are perfect candidates for sectioning. The Ford coupes from 1949 to 1951 were high on the list of good-looking customs. Their popularity continues in the current retro trend.

Cars were also lowered in the rear by de-arching the springs and using lowering blocks. Frame alterations such as C-ing and Z-ing were also common. Dropped axles, spindle-dropping kits, and repositioning the A-frame members were used to lower the front of the car. Suspension alterations could lower a car about 3 inches before it changed the ride to farm wagon quality—like the body was welded to the axles. How low could you go was a big challenge when building a custom, and the retro customs are slammed with the best of the originals. Air bag suspensions make it a bit easier today.

When cars are designed and built by the auto manufacturers they tend to have some concern for clear vision in all directions and comfortable seating positions. As a result, there is only so much that can be done to make a production car low and sleek. The customizers were free from such design restrictions because the right look was far more important than comfort. Therefore they could set new standards for cool, and by comparison the showroom cars looked tall and boxy. In addition to going low, it was just as important to make a custom unique in many ways.

Dressed to Kill

Fender skirts were practically mandatory on customs. Even though everyone did their own thing when building a custom, few could look the other way when it came to adding skirts. Whether they fit tight in the wheelwell or formed an elongated bubble over the rear quarter panel, skirts were "it" for the customs in the first 10 years or so after World War II.

Behind the skirts rolled big, fat whitewall tires that were barely visible. Up front was another story. The whitewall tires rolled in fully open wheelwells and were capped with the highest fashion in modern wheel disc covers. Although flipper-style wheel covers maintained the popularity they first gathered with the prewar customs, the flipper evolved into the spinner style.

The most sought-after spinner hubcaps belonged to the 1954 Olds Fiestas. The Fiesta was a limited-edition model, so the hubcaps were unique from the beginning. Eventually even the hot-rodders chose them for their cars. The Fiestas proved to be so popular that Olds soon made them an accessory wheel cover for all models. The main drawback to Fiestas was that the hubcaps would not stay on a car long. The combination of better-than-average foot

Tuck-and-roll upholstery was the clear-cut favorite in any early 1950s custom. Chrome window frames are another nice touch.

speed, a screwdriver, and darkness often took its toll. Because the demand continued to outstrip the supply, there are reproductions of the Fiesta spinner available now. A few of the other wheel discs that gained widespread popularity included the 1957 Dodge Lancer, 1956 Plymouth Fury, and the sombrero-style Cadillac models from 1955.

Developing a smooth style was another hallmark of the custom. One of the coolest and most common custom features was the shaved door handles. Handleless doors were

operated with strategically placed electric switches that activated solenoids, which "magically" opened doors and the trunk.

Frenched headlights were another almost standard treatment. When headlights are frenched, the headlight rims are welded to the fenders and leaded in so the headlights gain a slightly recessed appearance. After this treatment, any headlight adjustment or replacement unfortunately had to be accomplished from the rear through the fender well.

The same idea was also used on taillights. Manufacturers used taillight design to make a car distinctive at night. A custom car owner wanted nothing to do with brand identity, so taillights were modified or swapped entirely to create a mystery car that had the distinction of being like no other. Fenders were sometimes elongated and molded into the bodies to accommodate these modifications. Taillights from other makes, sometimes cut down or positioned upside down, were often substituted. Almost everything was tried. One of the easiest and most popular swaps for the shoebox Fords was replacing the stock taillights with the bullet-style lights from the mid-1950s Oldsmobile. As the manufacturers made taillights larger and more elaborate, these

bow ties. Extra ~~~
grille, pinstriping replaces ~
ornamentation, and Appelton s~
mounted on the cowl.

LEFT
A cool chop job gives this four-door 1953 Chevy much improved proportions. Fender skirts accentuate the lowered profile, and shaved door handles add to the smooth contours.

new lantern-like lamps were adapted for custom use on the older model cars. Extending the rear fenders and adapting taillights from a 1956 Chrysler, 1954 Mercury, or 1956 Lincoln each added a unique and handsome style. The most coveted taillights of this era were taken from the 1956 Packard.

The Grille of My Dreams

Swapping the original grilles with the grille (or pieces of the grille) from other cars provided another major step toward distinction, individuality, and personality. The stock grille on the 1949 to 1951 Mercs, one of the most admired customs of all time, were almost always replaced. A reworked 1954 Olds grille was one of the

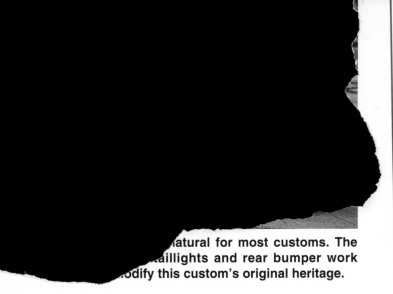

...atural for most customs. The ...aillights and rear bumper work ...odify this custom's original heritage.

RIGHT
**Just a few mild custom touches add distinctive-
ness to this 1947 Mercury convertible. Note the
recessed taillights and license plate. The pinstriping is subtle, as is the lowered suspension.**

good-looking alternatives, and mid-1950s
DeSoto grilles were also in demand. The
vertical grille bars from 1953 and 1954
Chevys were frequently used to customize
the grilles of other cars. It was also
common to add extra grille bars (referred
to as "teeth") to the stock Chevy grille.
The DeSoto grilles had a somewhat similar
toothy design that was frequently adapted
to other models.

When the 1954 Pontiac introduced the
floating center grille bar, it immediately
became a centerpiece for many customs,
especially the 1949 to 1951 Fords and 1949
to 1952 Chevys. Floating grilles were done
in many styles, but the effect was a grille bar
or grille ornamentation that appeared to be
structurally unattached to any framework. It

was created by using wire springs and
rubber pads. The design actually allowed
the grille to rebound when impacted, which
provided some degree of damage control.

Smooth . . . Real Smooth

One of the top customizers of that era,
Gene Winfield, was fond of adapting 1955
Pontiac front end cosmetics to the customs
he built. Winfield's shop was noted for
turning out beautiful customs based on the

72

1949–1952 Chevys. In most cases, the side trim and door handles were removed, and all the holes were filled. Winfield usually replaced the two-piece Chevy windshields with one-piece Oldsmobile units. He also tossed the original grilles, bumpers, and gravel shields. The body panels were either reshaped or new panels were added. To obtain a smooth overall appearance, Winfield preferred to mold in the hood and trunk.

Unique bumper styling was often done with the adaptation of bumpers from other cars and the creative use of bumper guards. The Kaiser three-piece units were a top choice. Good luck finding one today. In keeping with the desired smooth look, bumper bolts were shaved, welded, and filled for a seamless one-piece bumper appearance. Exiting the exhaust tips through the bumper ends was one of many custom styling features

that showed up on factory-built cars several years down the road.

The interiors of Winfield's customs were flashy. The instrument panel was painted and pinstriped or chromed or padded. Chrome plating was frequently added to the window frames, glove compartment door, kick panels, and heater cover. Seats were often recontoured and reupholstered—usually rolled and pleated with one of the new artificial leather fabrics such as Naugahyde. High-contrasting color combinations such as black and white, red and white, or blue and white were commonly selected. The headliners were elaborate and typically matched the seat upholstery material and design. Even the

A low profile and primer paint identifies the starting point for many of the retro customs being built today. In-progress customs are common at the retro rod shows. Spinner-style hubcaps and tunneled headlights indicate customizing intentions.

LEFT
One of the primary ideas behind building most rods and customs was to start with something inexpensive. For the retro custom enthusiast, an early 1950s Mopar is an alternative. Not only can you build a cool ride, but the unique factor goes way up.

interior of the trunk was often finished in matching upholstery.

Many customs were as much hot rod as they were custom. Engines were modified for increased horsepower, some to the extent of building full race engines. Like the hot-rodders, engine swapping was not uncommon. Lake pipes (exhaust pipes that followed the rocker panel area from just

behind the front wheel to just ahead of the rear wheel) had great appeal. Mufflers that produced a low, throaty growl, such as Smitty's, were big hits. Tachometers mounted on the steering column were yet another accessory.

By 1959, when the auto companies started building some flamboyant cars of their own, the customizers pushed the limits even further in order to stay ahead. As a result, customs became cartoonish and seemingly the work of science fiction illustrators. Imaginative design was never at a loss, but the world of customs changed immeasurably.

CHAPTER FOUR

For just about every retro rod being built and those already rollin' down the road, there is a person who belongs to a car club. The clubs are just as retro as the rods and customs that the members return to glory.

Car clubs proliferated in the 1950s. Their names were imaginative creations based on assorted car parts—Piston Jockeys, Hot Heads, and Gear Stretchers; mysterious clans or cliques—Arabs, Sheiks, and Night Prowlers; or gambling and the devil—Black Deuces, Eight Balls, and Lucky Devils. The members showed unity by wearing matching jackets with the club name across the back, and their rods and customs displayed club plaques mounted primarily on the bumpers or various other places.

During hot-rodding's formative years, the local clubs played an instrumental role in popularizing the sport. They provided, at the same time, a unique identity and a team quality; they were like different tribes within a hot rod nation. Each club expressed its individuality with its name and its particular style. While clubs took pride in their uniqueness, they shared a great deal with all the other hot rod clubs. In many areas, the local clubs joined to form larger groups in order to participate in organized racing. There were many such groups, but one of the oldest and most famous was the Southern California Timing Association (SCTA, formed in 1937), that formed the roots of the National Hot Rod Association in 1951.

San Diego–based Deacons hang together once or twice a week. All of the members, except one, are younger than 35 years old. Youthfulness is found among most retro rod club members.

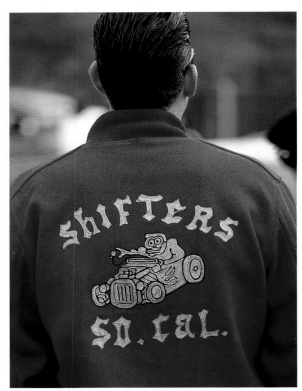

Being a club member requires involvement. It means helping to organize events and supporting the events of other clubs, as well as just hanging out with the guys and turning some wrenches. The cool jacket is just part of the deal.

LEFT
Club identification is noted on almost every retro rod. Most have rectangular plaques the size of a license plate. This cutout style badge is unique. It's not the plaque that makes a club cool. A club's reputation is based on the quality of its cars and members.

RIGHT
The cost of fuel is insignificant compared to the fun of being out on the road with your buddies. This is old-school hot-rodding at its best.

Retro rods are not just a guy thing. Chicks are always involved with the events, which include rockabilly music and swing dancing.

In the early 1950s many states considered laws to prohibit hot rods on the highways. Safety was a big issue due to the home-built nature of the cars and the emphasis on all-out speed. Potentially disastrous alterations to engines, suspensions, and running gear were not uncommon among the mechanically challenged shade tree mechanics. Some of these cars were clenched-teeth and wide-eyed fast, unmistakably dangerous, and driven irresponsibly. What was considered too fast, dangerous, and irresponsible had a wide degree of interpretation; however, it didn't take too many of these hot rod horrors before all rodders were painted with Satan's brush. The outlaw image often cast a nightmarish shadow, especially to those who were bothered by anyone who didn't care for Pat Boone.

Some car clubs promoted the rebel image and pushed it to its limits, others ignored whatever anyone thought about who they were or what they drove, and some even promoted safety and organized racing. Despite the popular perception that hot-rodders were dangerous and out of control, there were clubs that maintained basic safety regulations and car inspections with the idea that hot-rodding could be as safe as anyone wanted to make it.

Midnight racing all the way to Dead Man's Curve, with only one driver coming back to race again makes great movies

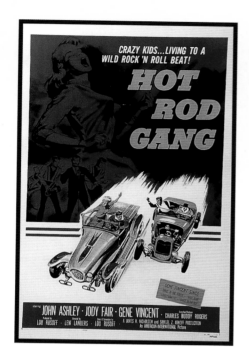

Publicity from 1950s-era films featuring hot rods can be found at almost every show, along with clothing and accessories for those who like to be immersed in the Custom Culture.

and folklore, but those occurrences probably happened less frequently than junior executives crashing their newly purchased fantasy cars right off the dealer showrooms. Stock engines were pumping out much more power than just a half dozen years earlier. Anyone who was young and into hot-rodding at that time will have death-defying stories—wrapped in truth, partial truth, and extemporaneous fabrication—about racing and wrecking. Danger, excitement, and varying degrees of a born-to-raise-hell attitude at times flowed as freely as 19-cents-a-gallon gasoline. It was part of the allure or the abhorrence, depending on your point of view.

Although street racing was important tribal warfare, and speed was status, there were many other aspects to rodding. Reliability runs were popular events that involved completing a predetermined course over public roads within a prescribed time frame. The courses were designed (more or less) to be traveled within the speed limits so high-speed driving was not a winning strategy. The best cars and drivers were able to compete at the closest possible time to a predetermined average speed. Rod runs, often involving many local car clubs, also became popular group activities. Various tests of driving skill were also dreamed up featuring obstacle courses and other

Red and white tuck and roll interiors, luxurious carpets, and ornate, 1950s-era steering wheels are some of the hot accessories found inside retro-style customs.

tricky closed-course routes. Each of these activities prompted participation and friendly competition.

The majority of the local clubs based membership on friendships, neighborhoods, and automotive loyalties. In the 1940s and 1950s, most of the clubs included both rods and customs. There was, in most cases, a mutual respect for each type of vehicle. Membership was granted rather than simply purchased, and club exclusivity was the reward. The same is true with the retro rod enthusiasts. The clubs were small and membership was exclusive. A really big club might have had 15 members, but 6 or 8 were more common. There are many similarities between today's retro rod clubs and those of 50 years ago—the club pride, camaraderie, interaction with other rod and custom clubs, and friendly competition.

The requirements to be a member of the Deacons, a San Diego retro rod and custom club, comes down to two basic qualifications: a common interest in the 1940s- and 1950s-style of building rods and customs and being the kind of person everybody else in the club likes to hang out with. Most of the Deacons, organized in 1977, started out with customs. The reason was mostly economic—a 1950s car is a lot less expensive than a 1930s car. You get more for your money. A young guy without much dough can afford a shoebox Ford or a fastback Chevy in rough condition. It's much

Pinstriping artists display incredible skills, even while people ask them questions and take their photos. Most shows have someone striping cars throughout the day.

easier to find a decent 1950s-era project car for less than $5,000 than it is to find a 1930s car from which to build a hot rod. The condition isn't always a high priority if the price is right; regardless of whether the custom is mild or wild, there is probably going to be some major bodywork done.

Vintage window decals add a little extra flavor. Performance parts, pin-up girls, racetrack memorabilia, and scenic destination decals are popular accessory items that are for sale at most events.

The Deacons started out with six like-minded hot-rodders; four of them had split off from an existing club that had grown too large. "The idea is to have everyone in the club participate," says Jonny Guilmet, one of the founding Deacons. The reason he and several others left their previous club was because they were the core group that did everything together. A club that has nonparticipants is no club at all to their way of thinking. The Deacons hang out together once or twice a week, help each other with their cars, and travel to shows together.

The mainstream car clubs that have dozens, hundreds, or even thousands of members usually rely on a small, core group that does most of the work organizing shows, cruises, and other events. Typically the core members are the ones involved with exchanging technical information and lending a hand with mechanical and restoration problems. The majority of members in a large club go along for the ride. With a large club there are frequently divisions and rifts that work against the collective purpose. Keeping a club small and exclusive to those who want to participate and be involved builds strong club loyalty. "You can't just hand a plaque and jacket to everyone," Guilmet says. "If you just try to build the numbers, and not everyone is friends, it just doesn't work."

No dues. No official meetings. No slackers. For many of the retro rod and custom clubs it's that simple, straightforward, and direct. It's a brotherhood of sorts. Clubs consist of people you can count on and who want to be part of the fun. Member number seven of the Deacons joined about a month after the club first came together, but in the past three years, only two more members were voted in.

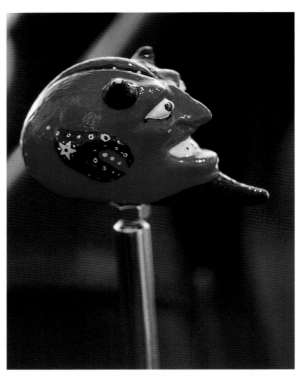

This devil head shifter knob is a cool item, particularly if your club has a name like the Lucky Devils.

RIGHT
This 1932 three-window coupe awaits attention in the shop at the Don Garlits Museum in Florida. Garlits plans to use it as his personal car.

Traditionally rods and customs were built for the street. Building high-dollar versions for show was something that evolved throughout the 1950s and took the hobby in another direction in the 1960s and on into the future. Because retro-rodding is youth-oriented, there is more interest placed on driving than showing what they've built.

PREVIOUS PAGE
The NHRA California Hot Rod Reunion in Bakersfield, California, is a celebration of drag racing history and a destination for many of the highly mobile retro-rodders.

To contribute to the club, it's necessary that the members live close by each other to attend the unofficial regular meetings for garage work or just hanging out. Some clubs have a central garage where members congregate and get most of the work done. One member may have the available space for projects, but things like garage space are fleeting, and shop space for club project cars likely will change. The talents are usually spread throughout the club as well. Even the small clubs probably have at least one member who is skilled at engine work, another who knows bodywork, maybe one member is a painter, or one has special skills that everyone else benefits from. For instance, some guys may not have the mechanical abilities, but they beat the bushes to find the parts that other members need for their cars. The point is that everybody contributes. It's a team effort and the enthusiasm is contagious. "The more you hang out," Guilmet says, "the more you learn about the old stuff and how cool it is. We all have projects in the wind waitin' to be put together."

restorations. Because it's more about participation than perfection, the cars at retro rod shows are likely to be works in progress. Conversations are as often about what's next in the building process, or what parts are needed or have been recently found. Cars in two or three shades of primer, and even in bare metal with the scars of recent metal cutting and welds, are on the road and headed to the next show. Some look like they would be lucky to make it across town much less hundreds of miles.

In southern California, there are retro-rodding events happening pretty much monthly. Individual clubs sponsor one or two each year, and anywher̄ between 50 and 150 retro rods and show up. The best of the retro ro ̄id each Memorial Day weekend in ̄mall central California town of Paso Robles, located on Highway 101. Retro-rodders throughout the West refer to the annual pilgrimage as simply "Paso." Downtown Paso Robles has a park in the main square where hundreds of rods and customs are spread out underneath tall, shady trees. The streets around the square are also jammed with the coolest rods and customs. Up and down Highway 101 the cruise is constant. Friday night there is a huge parade with thousands of people, mostly locals, lining the streets. The event has become so popular that a second meet has been organized for the Labor Day weekend, and the numbers of rods and customs in attendance is equal to

Young people having fun with old cars is not very common among car hobbyists in general, at least not in the same numbers as the young people who are drawn to the retro rods and customs.

what the Memorial Day event was drawing just a few years ago.

The Paso Robles show began in the mid-1980s when the West Coast Kustoms car club had the idea for an annual get-together. During the past several years the Memorial Day Paso Robles show grown dramatically, which serves as a gauge for the increasing popularity of the retro rods and customs. The fact that a growing contingent of young people with some sense of hot rod history are fueling this and making it a participatory event is unique within the old-car hobby.

Another major retro-rodding event is Viva Las Vegas, which takes place in March at the Gold Coast Casino and Hotel in Las Vegas. It attracts more than 125 rods and customs, even though it is a grueling drive across the desert to get there from almost anywhere. For the rodders it's a challenge to drive there. The weather is unpredictable and the route includes some long and steep mountain grades.

Retro-rodding is full of challenges and adventures, but the bottom line is still the same as it's always been: hanging out and having fun.

Visually, a couple of cars travel more than 2,500 miles to attend, but the majority comes from a 300- to 500-mile radius of Las Vegas. Once they all converge, the top floor of the Gold Coast's parking garage looks like double-feature night at the Western Sky drive-in theater.

Credit for pulling off this show and mixing it in with a gigantic rockabilly weekend primarily goes to the Shifters, an Orange County, California,-based retro rod club. Viva Las Vegas attracts worldwide attention. It's promoted in Europe, Australia, and Japan, but its content is full-bore Americana. The round-the-clock rockabilly music is a huge attraction for many young kids who are embracing the 1950s nostalgia as a lifestyle that's been labeled "Custom Culture." Music, clothing, art, and 1950s memorabilia are all part of the show. Among the famous attendees at the 2000 show were Rat Fink artist Ed "Big Daddy" Roth, custom car–building legend Gene Winfield, and Paul le Mat, the actor who played John Milner in the movie *American Graffiti*. The famous Milner Coupe, arguably the most recognized hot rod of all time, from the movie was also on hand at the 2000 show.

The big shows like these provide fantastic gatherings of rods and customs;

Although there's no easy way to drive there, car clubs from throughout the West caravaned their rods and customs to the Viva Las Vegas show and rockabilly weekend. The Shifters, from Orange County, California, organized the event.

however, they also shift the attention away from the essence of the hobby and turn it into more of a spectacle. One of the guys from the Choppers car club based in Burbank, California, surveyed the situation at Viva Las Vegas and said, "If there weren't big events being held for the '50s-style rod and custom enthusiasts, the Choppers would just be meeting in a parking lot somewhere on a Friday night to share stories about what they've done or are doing to their rods." It's not about fashion and following a trend. It's all about hanging out and digging these cars.

Although there is a lone wolf and rebellious youth image ingrained in hot-rodding, among the young retro-rodders there is also a strong connection to the history of rodding. Many of the rodders have family ties that go back at least a generation, mostly to fathers who raised

There's no shortage of help when car repairs need to be made at a rod and custom show. Viva Las Vegas is one of the West's biggest and most entertaining retro rod shows.

them around hot rods. Vivid childhood memories of riding in Dad's rod are still fresh and, when you ask them, recollections come to mind quickly. Spending time with Dad in the garage made some durable impressions. A father helping his son build a rod for his first car is a story that will be retold many times over the years.

Now the experience is being passed along as another generation is being raised on the old-school rods and customs. They'll have similar fond memories 25 years down the road. There's a far greater family aspect to hot-rodding than a lot of people outside the hobby would imagine. You see it in the frequent picnic-type gatherings that many of the clubs sponsor. As one rodder told me, "You really have to prioritize your life to be able to do this—come to these things and have a care. You make a lot of sacrifices. I got a wife and kids and it gets hard sometimes to do this. When you get really involved, you find the dedication requires a time factor and the money factor."

There's a commitment that affects the whole family, which is probably why it becomes a family activity for those who are really into it. With dedication like that it's not surprising that attention to detail is important to so many.